# SUPER STEAM

## ACTIVITY BOOK

### Launch Learning with Fun Mazes, Dot-to-Dots, Search-the-Page Puzzles, and More!

**Mandisa Watts**

ROCKRIDGE
PRESS

To my little artist, engineer, and scientist—Zola, Nayla, and Asher.

For general information on our other products and services or to obtain technical support, please contact our Customer Care Department within the United States at (866) 744-2665, or outside the United States at (510) 253-0500.

Rockridge Press publishes its books in a variety of electronic and print formats. Some content that appears in print may not be available in electronic books, and vice versa.

TRADEMARKS: Rockridge Press and the Rockridge Press logo are trademarks or registered trademarks of Callisto Media Inc. and/or its affiliates, in the United States and other countries, and may not be used without written permission. All other trademarks are the property of their respective owners. Rockridge Press is not associated with any product or vendor mentioned in this book.

Interior and Cover Designer: Mando Daniel
Art Producer: Tom Hood
Editor: Elizabeth Baird
Production Editor: Mia Moran
Production Manager: Martin Worthington

Illustration © Collaborate Agency/Elsa Grieve 2020

ISBN: Print 978-1-64876-864-4
R0

# Note to Caregivers

Welcome to the *Super STEAM Activity Book*! My name is Mandisa Watts and I am the founder of Happy Toddler Playtime, an online resource for caregivers showcasing child-led learning activities. I'm also the author of *Exciting Sensory Bins for Curious Kids*. My specialty is creating fun activities for kids centered around science, literacy, and math.

STEAM stands for science, technology, engineering, arts, and mathematics. STEAM is vital in early childhood education because it gives children the foundation to explore, question, and discover the world around them. Research also shows that exposure to STEAM concepts early on has a positive impact on children's perception and disposition toward STEAM subjects in the future.

This book contains tons of activities that will keep kids engaged and entertained, like mazes, dot-to-dots, coloring activities, spot-the-difference puzzles, and more. Accompanying each activity is a simplified explanation of a STEAM-related concept, like what atoms are, why levers are useful, or how airplanes fly. While working through the activities, your child will develop their reading and fine motor skills; strengthen their knowledge of colors, numbers, and shapes; improve their concentration and confidence; and, most of all, develop a positive association with STEAM.

There is no right way to work through this book. Your child can do the activities in order or simply do what appeals to them. Either way, get ready for some STEAM-themed fun!

# Super
# Science Fun

# Thirsty Trees

Trees need water to live. They get water from their roots, which are underground. Solve the maze to help the water find its way up the roots to the tree.

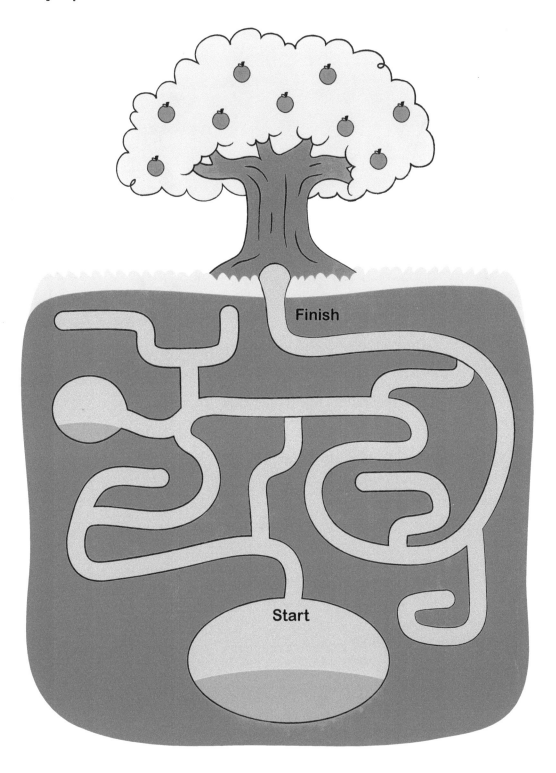

# Dino Differences

Dinosaurs were some of the biggest animals to ever live on Earth. They lived long before humans. Which dinosaur is different from the rest?

A.

B.

C.

D.

# Stellar Solar System

There are eight planets in our solar system. Circle the planet that comes next in each pattern.

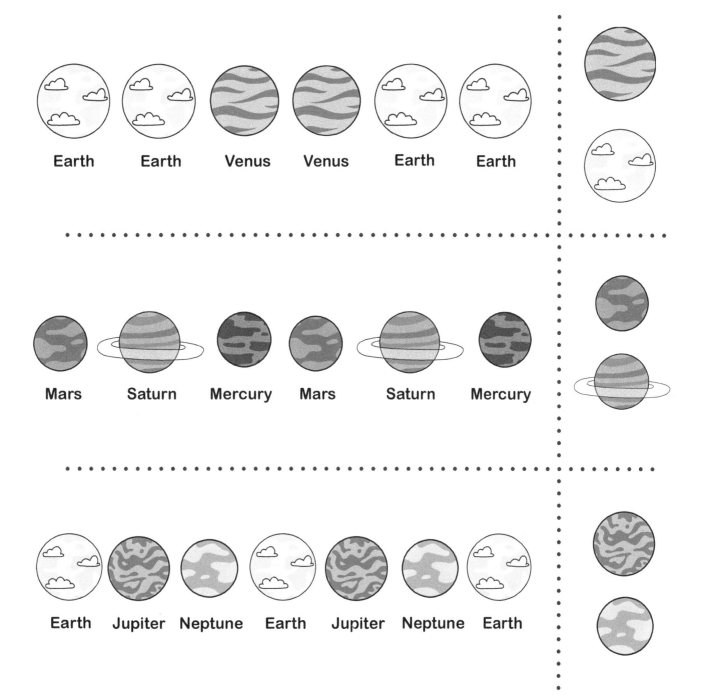

Earth    Earth    Venus    Venus    Earth    Earth

Mars    Saturn    Mercury    Mars    Saturn    Mercury

Earth   Jupiter   Neptune   Earth   Jupiter   Neptune   Earth

# Friendly Fish

Marine biology is the study of ocean life. Use the number key to color the fish.

# Find the Liquids

Liquids flow and take the shape of whatever they are placed in. Water is a common liquid. Circle the liquids below.

Puppy

Juice

Milk

Garbage Truck

Apple

Soup

# End of the Rainbow

Rainbows are formed when light shines through water, like when the sun shines through rain. Finish the picture of the rainbow.

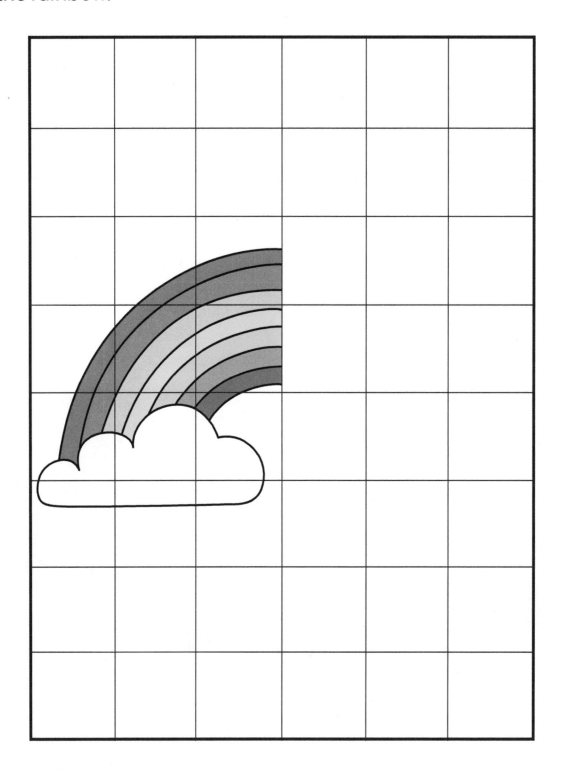

# Funny Bones

Your body is made up of bones. They give your body its shape and help you move. Connect the dots to discover a skeleton.

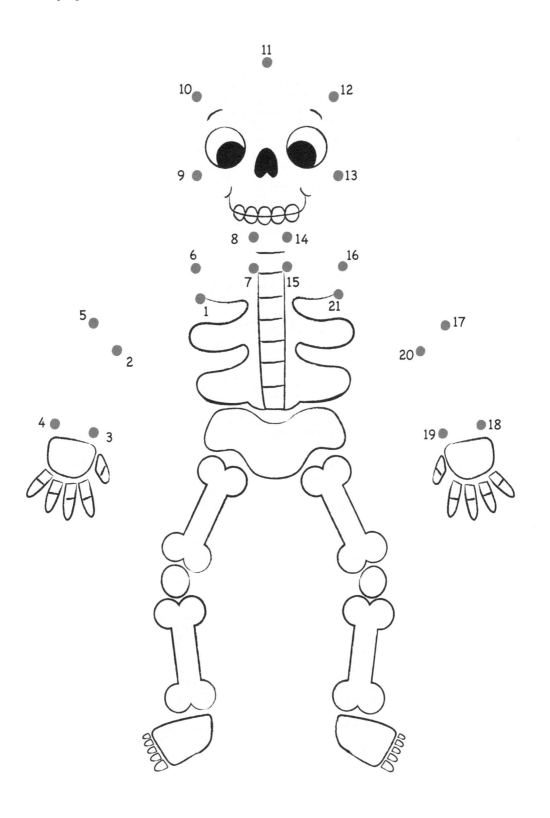

# Happy Habitats

A habitat is where a plant or animal lives. Which pond habitat is different from the rest?

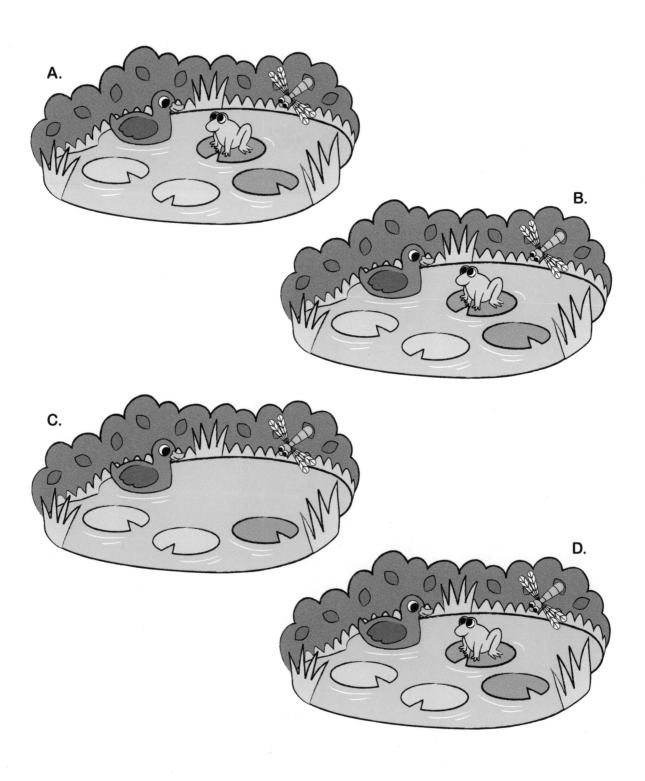

A.

B.

C.

D.

# The LEGOs of the Universe

Atoms are tiny particles that make up all the stuff we can see, like this activity book! Use the letter key to color the picture.

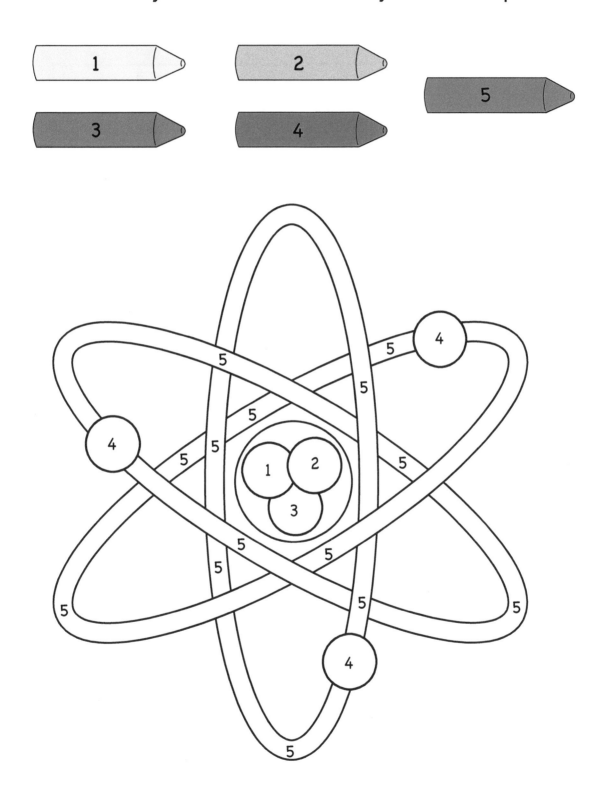

# Up, Up, and Away!

Air rises when it gets hotter, which can make balloons float. Finish the picture of the hot-air balloon.

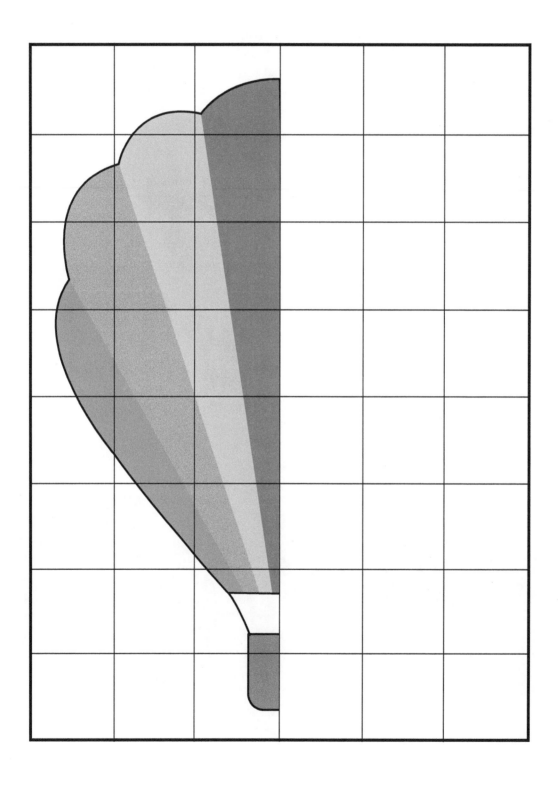

# Growing Tall

Flowers need water and sunlight to grow. Connect the dots to see what is growing in the pot.

# Search the Science Lab

Scientists work in places called laboratories. Find the following objects in the laboratory below:

**Calculator**  **Notebook**  **Test Tubes**  **Goggles**  **Microscope**  **Beaker**

# Super Technology Fun

# Cyber Connections

The Internet connects computers all over the world! Help connect these two computers on opposite sides of the world.

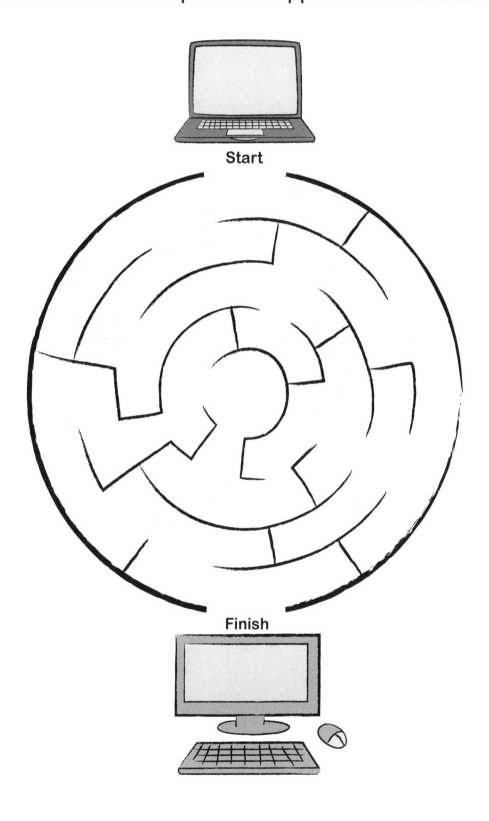

Start

Finish

# Which Car Is Different?

A self-driving car can drive by itself! Which self-driving car is different from the rest?

A.

B.

C.

D.

# 3D Printer Magic

A 3D printer can print objects like furniture, tools, and toys.
Circle the toy that comes next in each pattern.

# Fast Trains

Some high-speed trains can travel up to 160 miles per hour!
Use the number key to color the high-speed train.

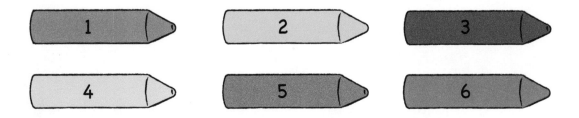

# Wireless World

Wireless technology lets electronics talk to each other without using wires to connect. Circle the electronics that use wireless technology.

Cell Phone

Toothbrush

Coat

Printer

Headphones

Swing

# Sun Power

Solar panels make electricity from sunlight. Finish the picture of the sun.

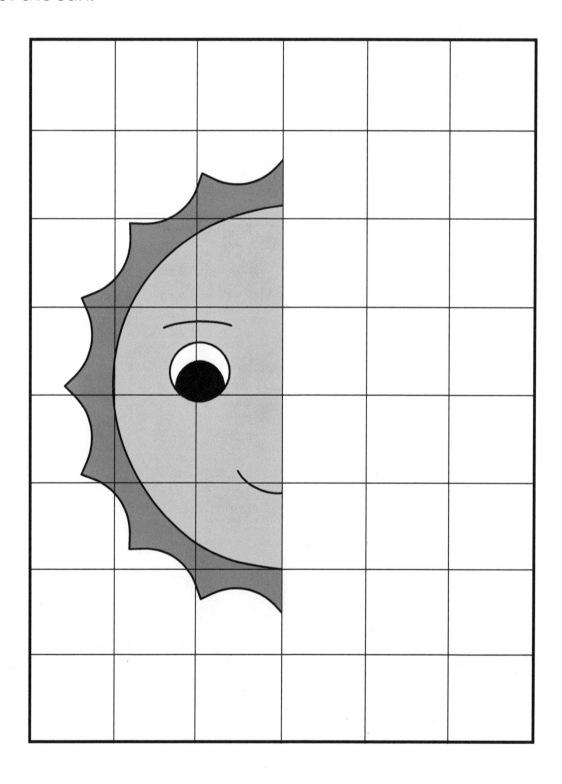

# Farm Helpers

Farm robots help with farm work like planting, harvesting, and weeding. Connect the dots to see what is helping on the farm.

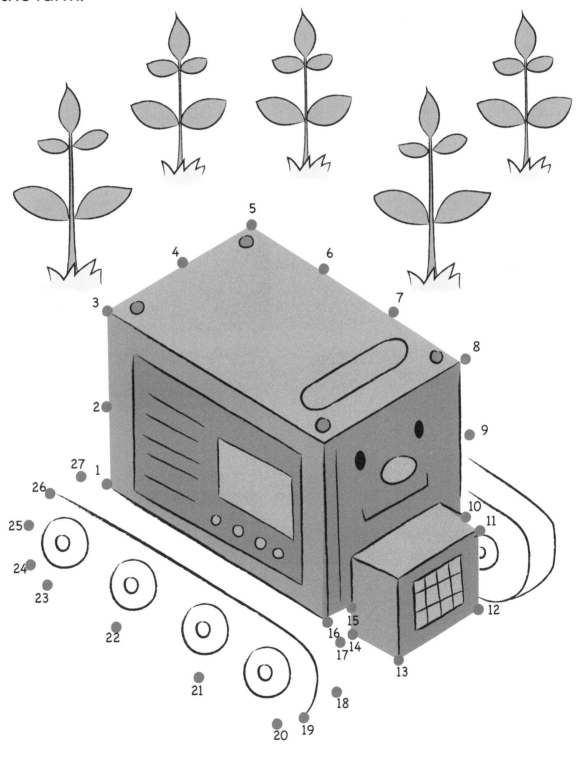

# Beautiful Binary

Binary is the language of computers. Instead of the alphabet, computers use 0s and 1s to talk to each other. Which binary code is different from the rest?

A. 0110100001101001

B. 0110100001101001

C. 0110100001101001

D. 111111111111111111111111

# Robots in Space

Space robots are called rovers. Scientists send them to other planets to collect information. Help the rover travel around Mars.

# Find Your Way

A compass is one of the oldest technologies. It helps us find directions—north, south, east, and west—by pointing the arrow at N, S, E, or W. Circle the direction that comes next in each pattern.

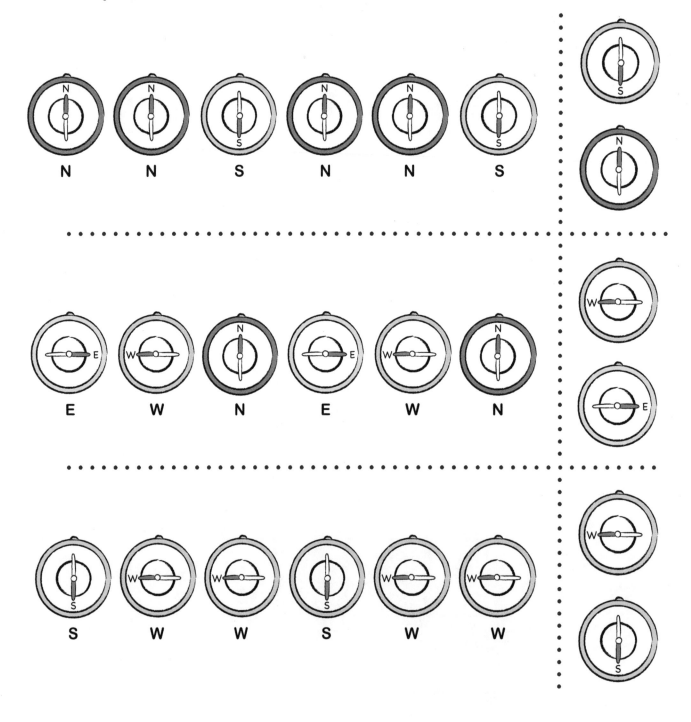

N    N    S    N    N    S

E    W    N    E    W    N

S    W    W    S    W    W

# Clever Robots

Artificial intelligence (AI) is how robots and computers learn.
Color the robot by following the letters.

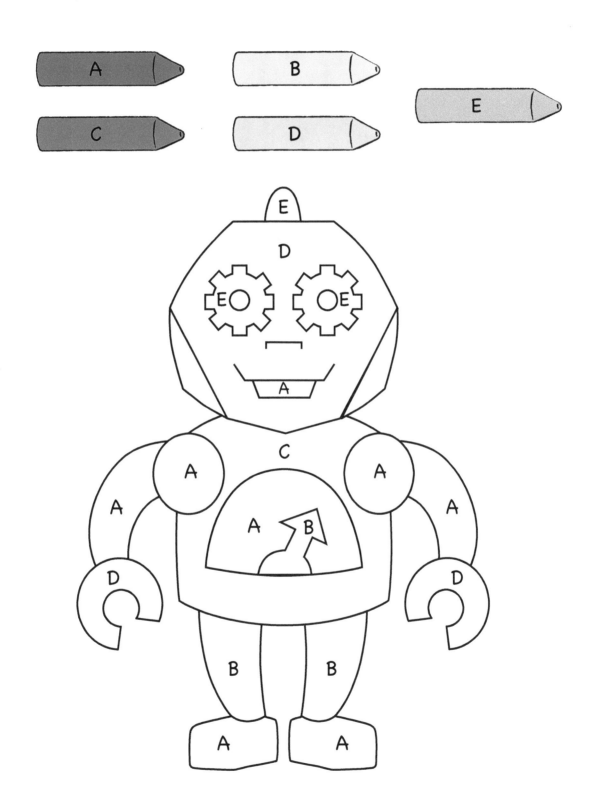

# Search the Computer Lab

Computers are made up of monitors, keyboards, and processors. Find the following objects in the computer lab picture below:

**Processor**

**Mouse**

**Headphones**

**Cables**

**Speakers**

**Printer**

# Super Engineering Fun

# Land the Drone

Drones are flying robots! Help the drone go through the maze to land safely on the landing pad.

Start

Finish

# Equipment Engineers

Sports engineers create equipment like helmets and padding that keep players safe. Can you spot the difference in one of the pictures?

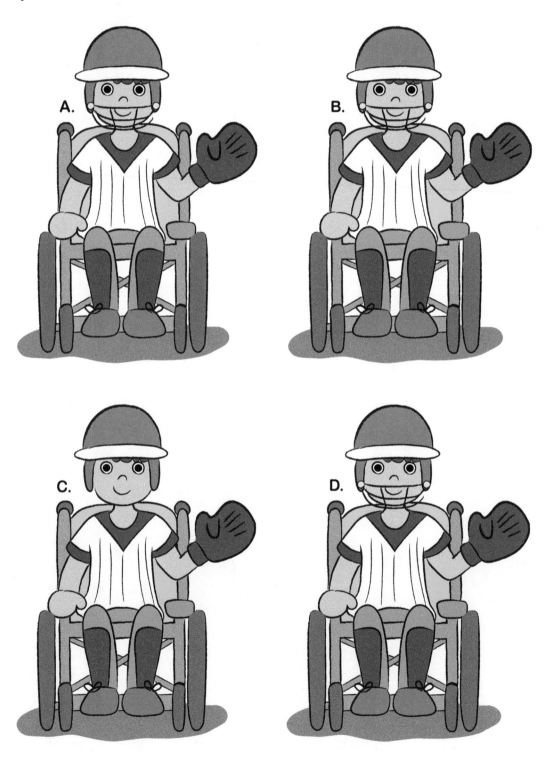

# Wings Up

Airplane wings push air downward, which helps planes fly.
Circle the airplane that comes next in each pattern.

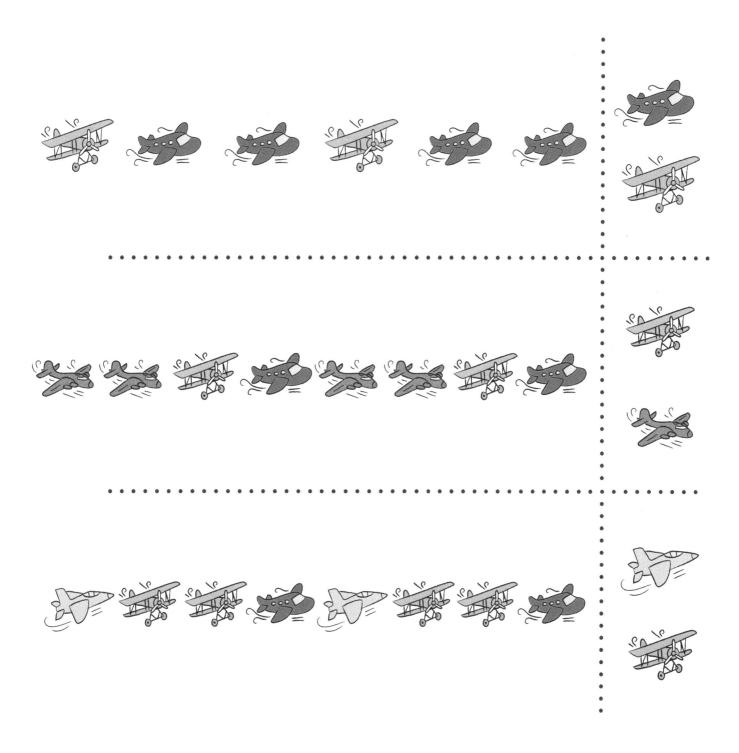

# Incredible Parachutes

A parachute slows down an object falling toward the ground.
Use the shape key to color the parachute.

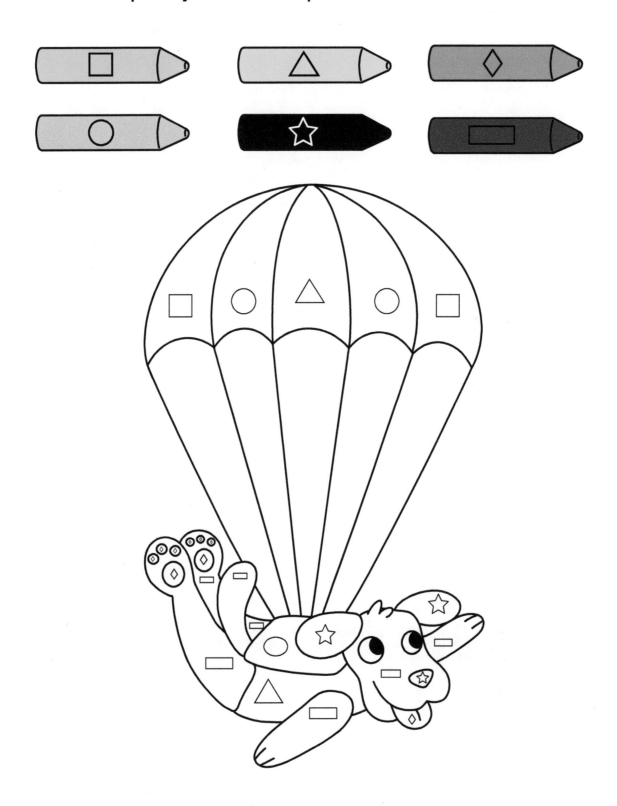

# Which Use Ropes?

Ropes and cables have a lot of tensile strength. That means it takes a lot to break them. Circle the items that use ropes or cables.

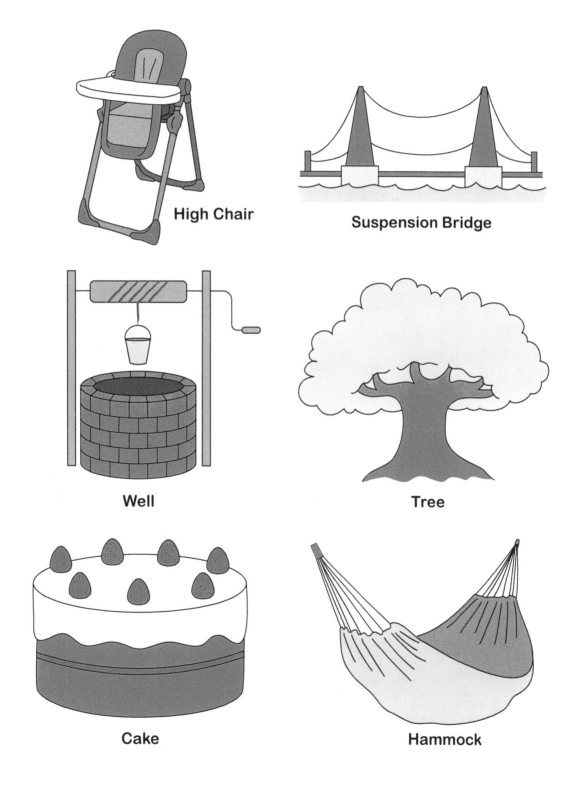

High Chair

Suspension Bridge

Well

Tree

Cake

Hammock

# Amazing Arches

Arches are curved openings that can support the weight of bridges and buildings. Finish the picture of the arch.

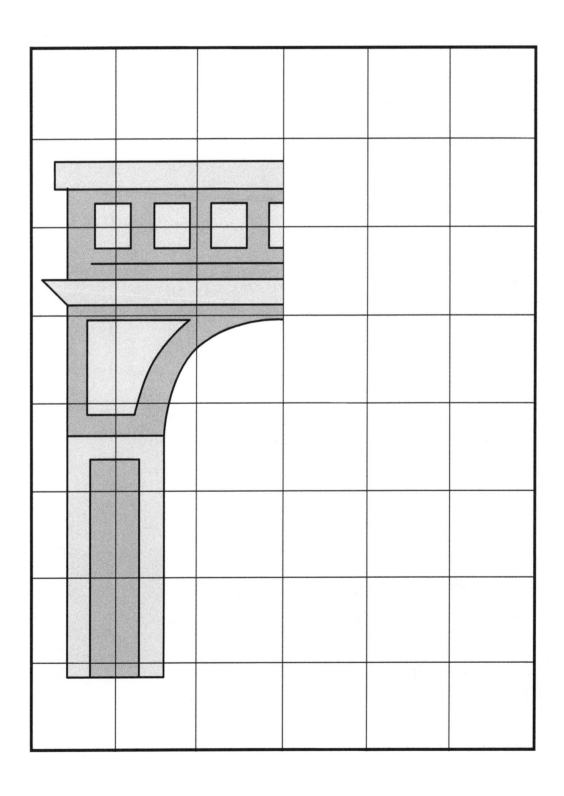

# Gear Up and Go

Gears on a bicycle move power from the pedals to the wheels. Connect the dots to see the gears.

# Stop Your Engines

Gravity is an invisible force that pulls objects toward each other. Roller coasters use it to move along tracks. Help the roller coaster car ride through the maze.

Start

Finish

# Playground Engineering

Levers, like seesaws, are simple machines that can lift heavy objects. Circle the picture that looks different than the rest.

A.

B.

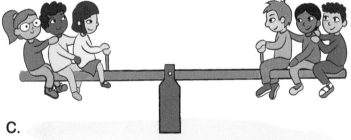

C.

D.

# On the Construction Site

Construction sites are full of big machines that help move heavy objects. Circle the machine that comes next in each pattern.

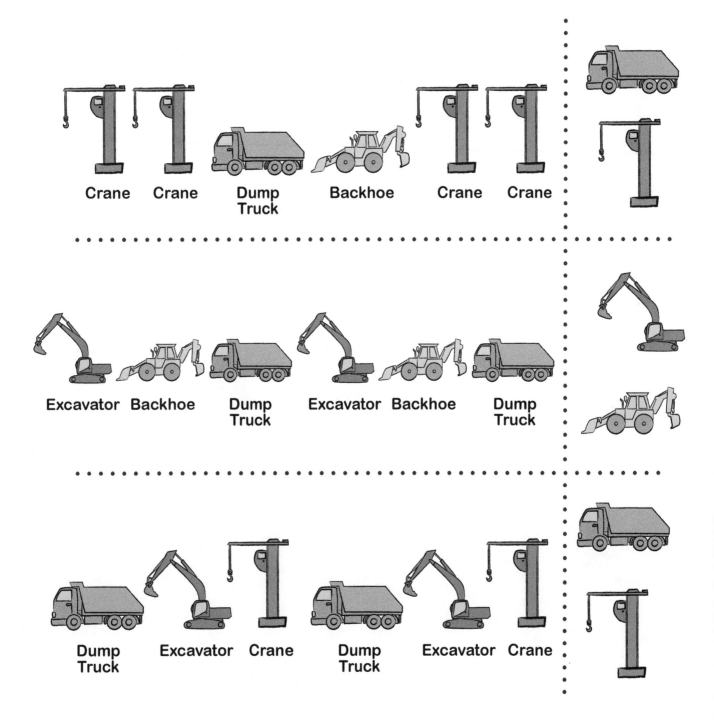

Crane  Crane  Dump Truck  Backhoe  Crane  Crane

Excavator  Backhoe  Dump Truck  Excavator  Backhoe  Dump Truck

Dump Truck  Excavator  Crane  Dump Truck  Excavator  Crane

# Blast Off!

To leave Earth and enter space, rockets must go very fast. Gases coming out of the nozzle push the rocket up so it can blast off! Use the number key to color the rocket ship.

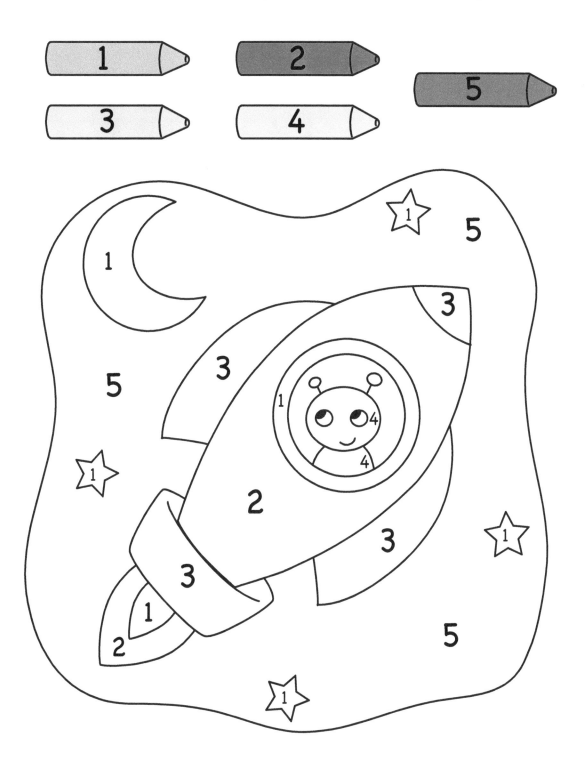

# Search the Ocean

Submarines use sonar, or sound waves, to find their way through dark oceans, just like whales and dolphins! Find the following items in the under-the-sea picture below:

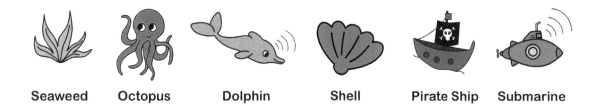

Seaweed   Octopus   Dolphin   Shell   Pirate Ship   Submarine

# Super Art Fun

# Theater Maze

A theater is a place where people go to see plays and other performances. Help the people find their seats in the theater.

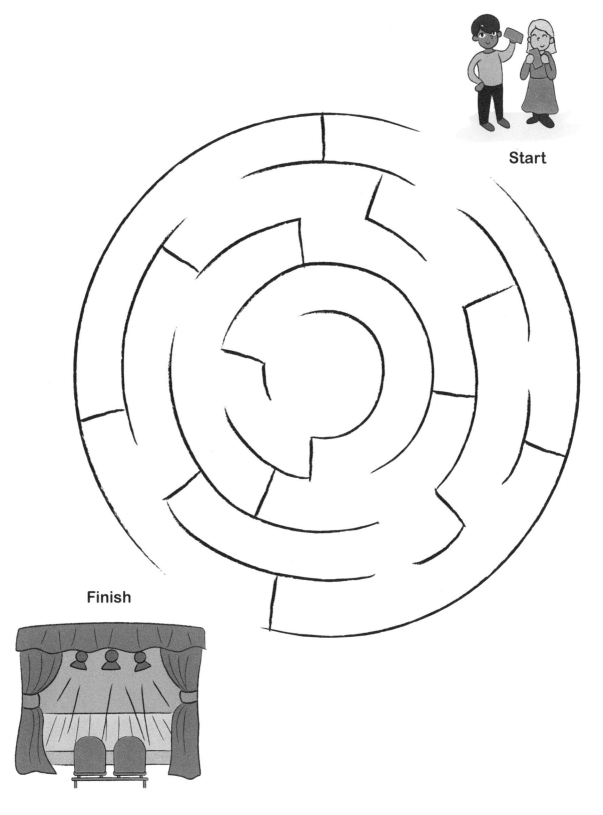

Start

Finish

# Priceless Pottery

Ceramic vases were first used to carry water. They can also be works of art, because of their beautiful shapes and paintings. Find which vase is different from the other three below.

A.

B.

C.

C.

# Artful Buildings

Architecture is the art and science of designing buildings like houses and schools. Circle the building that comes next in each pattern.

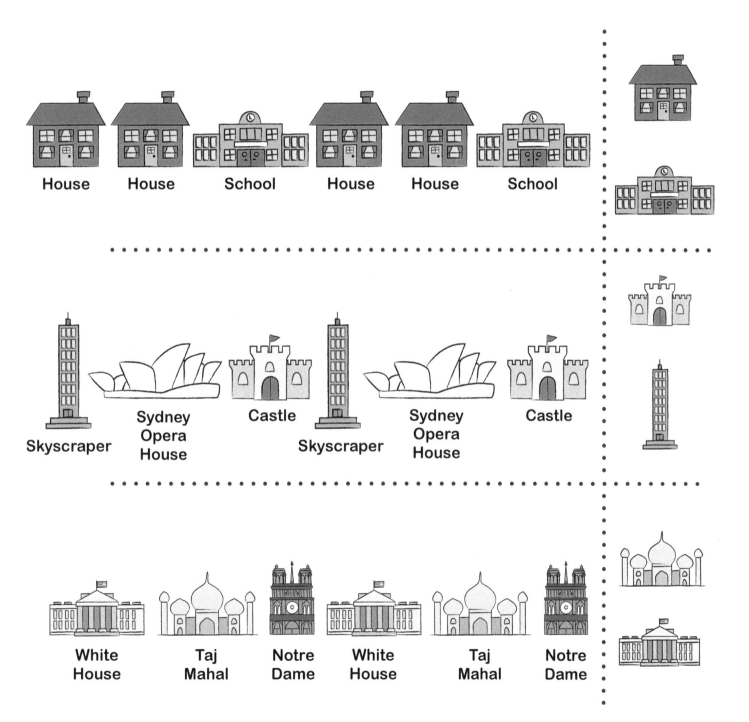

House   House   School   House   House   School

Skyscraper   Sydney Opera House   Castle   Skyscraper   Sydney Opera House   Castle

White House   Taj Mahal   Notre Dame   White House   Taj Mahal   Notre Dame

# Lovely Landscapes

Landscape paintings show scenes from the outdoors. Use the number key to color the landscape.

# Which Have Strings?

Stringed instruments make sounds by vibrating strings with your hand or a bow. Circle the stringed instruments below.

Violin

Lion

Guitar

Fire Truck

Fish

Harp

# Splendid Sculptures

Sculpture is an art form that involves molding stone or clay into any shape you want. Connect the dots to discover a sculpture of a horse.

# Finish the Piano

The piano is a very complicated musical instrument. It has more than 12,000 parts, including 88 keys. Finish the picture of the piano.

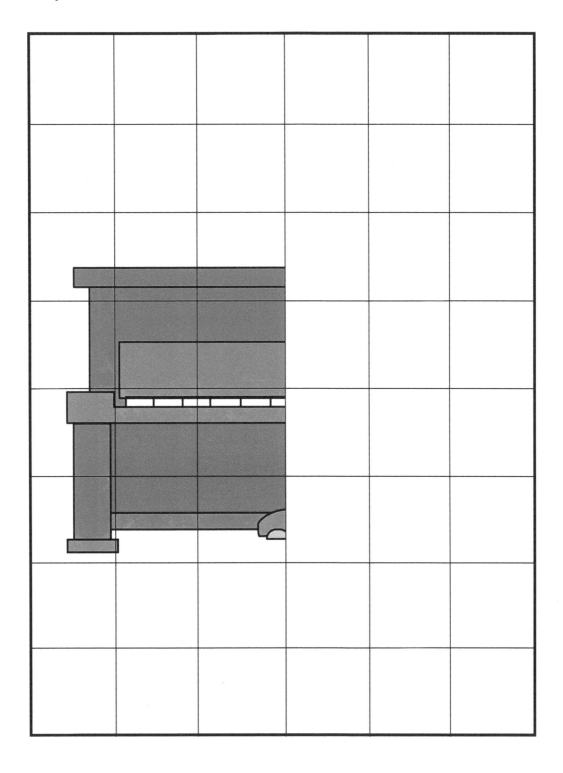

# Beautiful Ballet

Ballet is a graceful form of dance that brings stories to life through movement. Follow the pattern ● ● to help the ballerina find her shoes.

# Grand Opera

An opera is like a play where the characters sing their lines.
Can you spot the difference in one of the pictures?

A.

B.

C.

D.

# Creative Composers

A composer writes music for things like movies and computer games. Circle the musical symbol or note that comes next in each pattern.

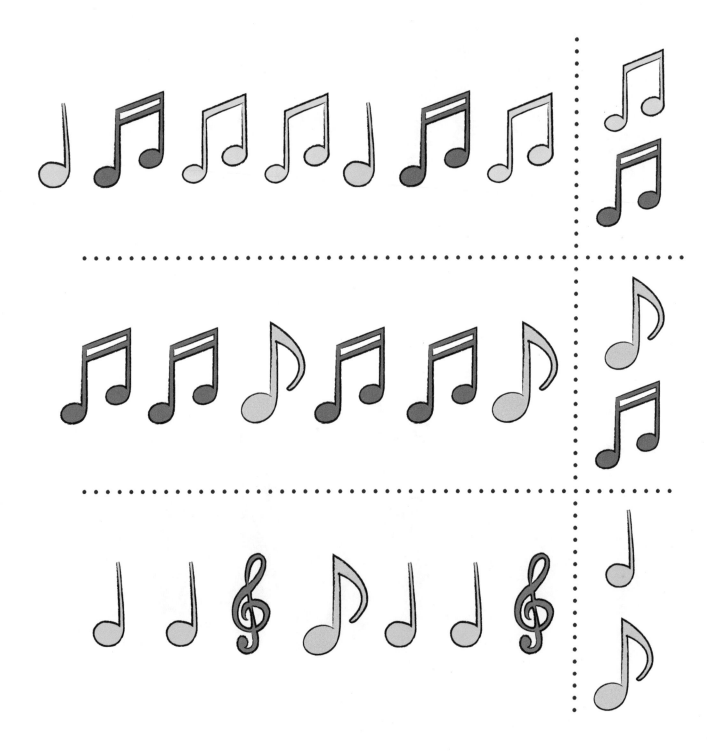

# B-Girl Style

Break dancing is a form of dance that involves athletic movements, coordination, and style. Connect the dots to discover the break-dancer.

# Search the Gallery

An art gallery is a place where you can see works of art. Find the following objects in the picture:

Book     Guide     Rope     Vase     Sculpture     Painting     Chair

# Super Math Fun

# 1, 2, 3, Go!

Follow the path with the pattern 1, 2, 3, to help the race car find the finish line.

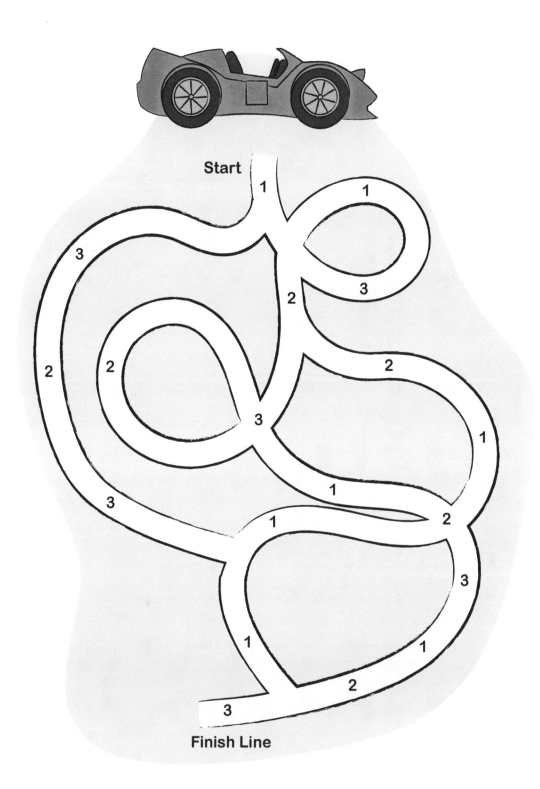

Start

Finish Line

# Count the Squirrels!

Let's count to 5: 1, 2, 3, 4, 5! Circle the park that has 5 squirrels.

A.

B.

C.

D.

# 3D Shapes

3D shapes are everywhere! Birthday hats are cones. Balls are spheres. Blocks are cubes. Cans are cylinders. Circle the 3D shape that comes next in each pattern.

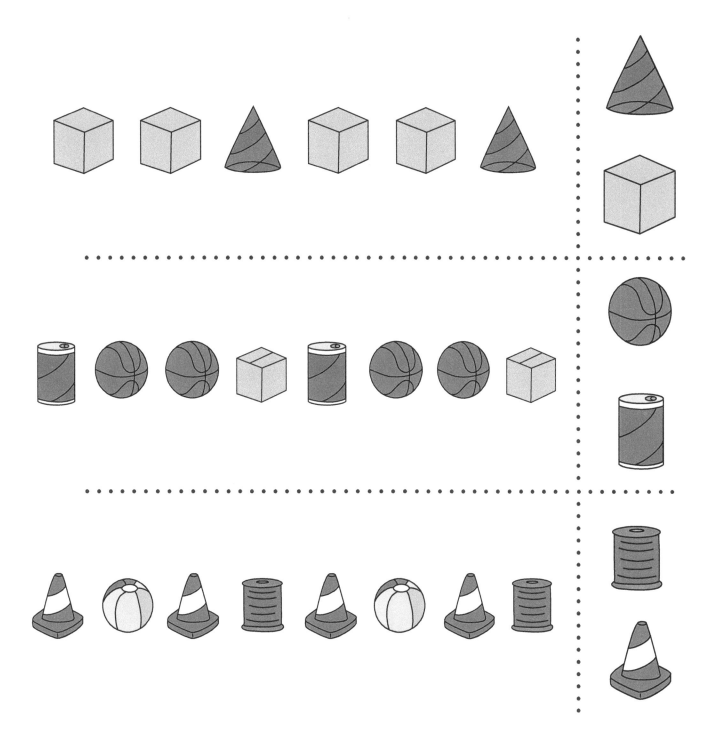

# Graph It!

Graphs are drawings that turn numbers into information you can see. Use the number key to color the graph.

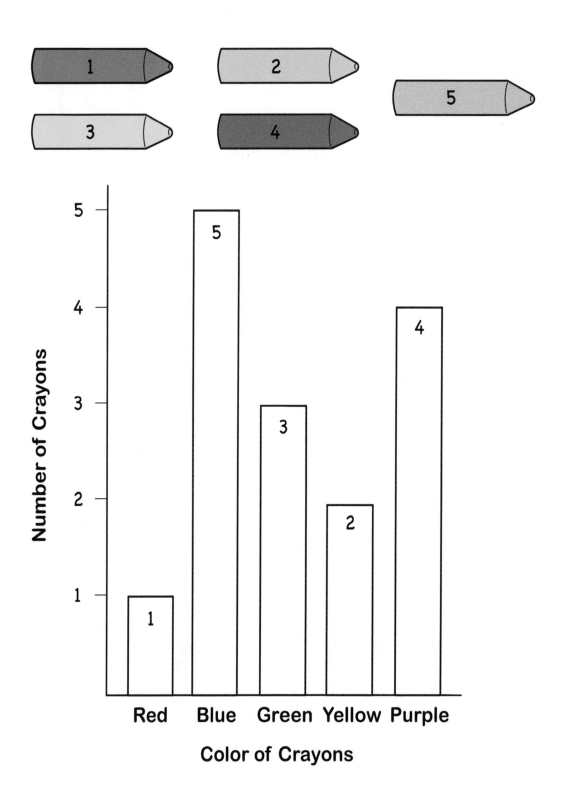

# Rad Rulers

Rulers and tape measures are tools used to measure how long something is. Circle the items that are used for measuring length.

Tape Measure

Lawn Mower

Hammer

Watering Can

Ruler

# Mirror Image

Something is symmetrical when it is the same on both sides. It's like a mirror image! Finish the other side of the ladybug to make it symmetrical.

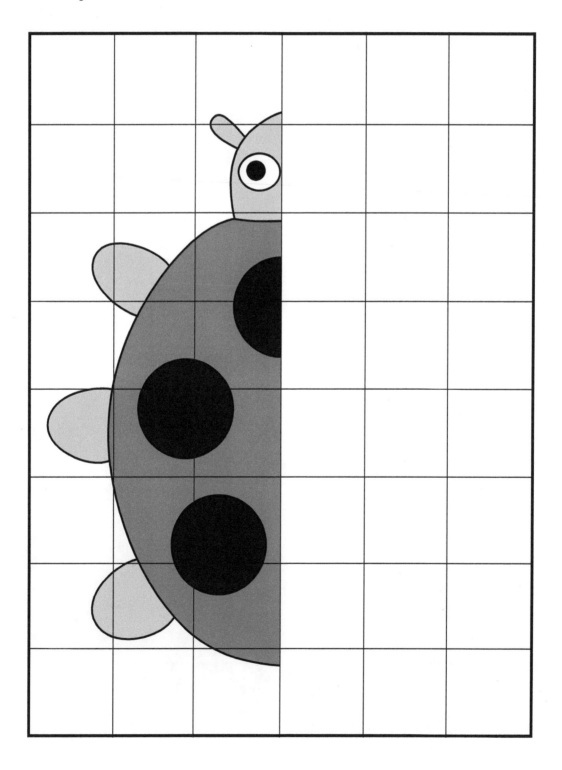

# Awesome Angles

When two straight lines meet, they form an angle. Connect the dots to discover a star with many angles.

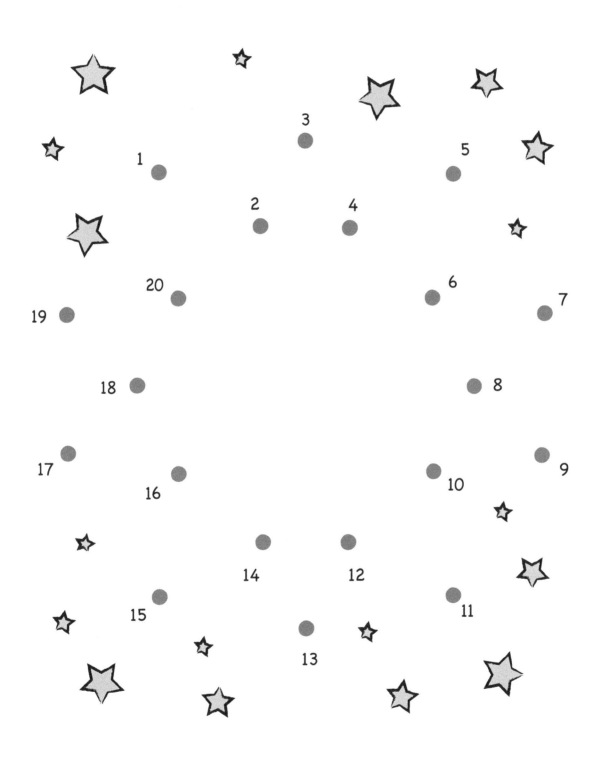

# Let's Go Fishing

Let's count to 15: 1, 2, 3, 4, 5, 6, 7, 8, 9, 10, 11, 12, 13, 14, 15!
Follow the numbers in order from 1 to 15 to help the kids find
the lake and go fishing.

# Fun with Fractions

A fraction is a part of something whole. For example, a slice of cake is a fraction of a whole cake. Circle the cake with the biggest fraction missing!

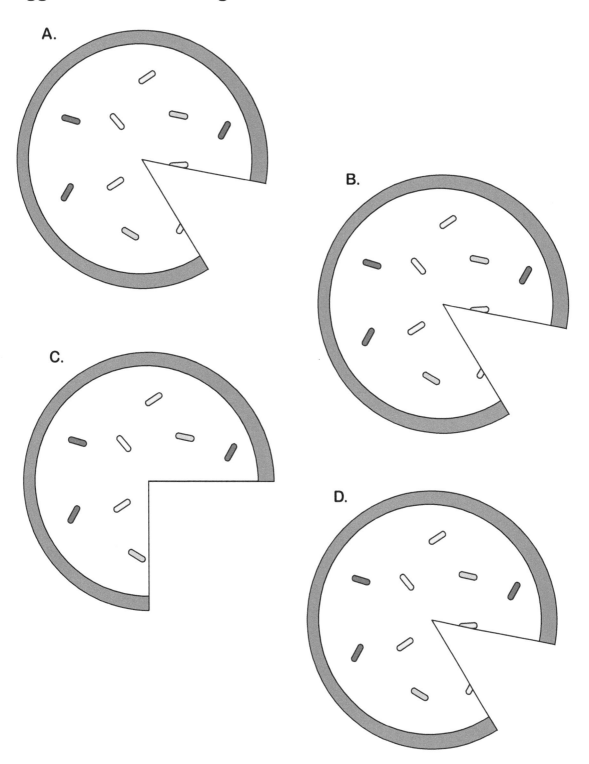

A.

B.

C.

D.

# Money Matters

Money comes in different shapes and colors depending on how much it is worth. Circle the coin or bill that comes next in each pattern.

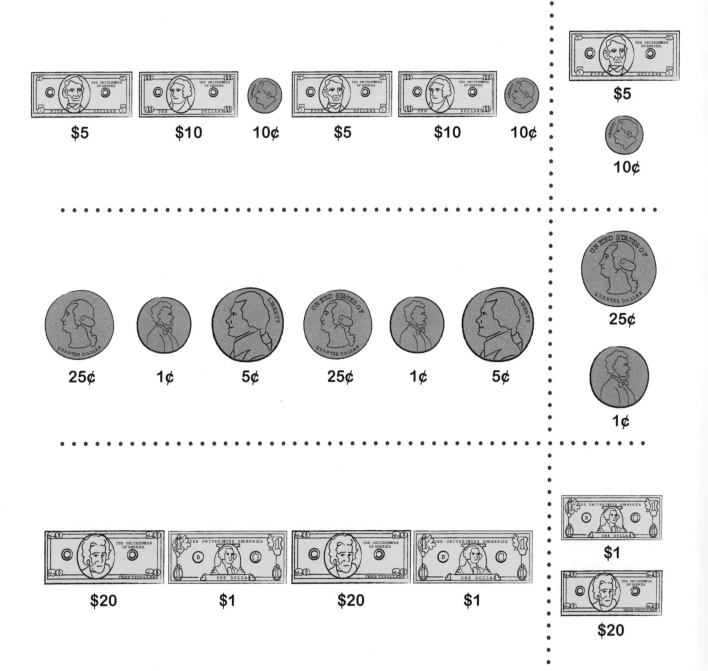

# Countdown!

Let's count backwards! 10, 9, 8, 7, 6, 5, 4, 3, 2, 1. Follow the path that counts backwards from 10 to 1 to finish the maze.

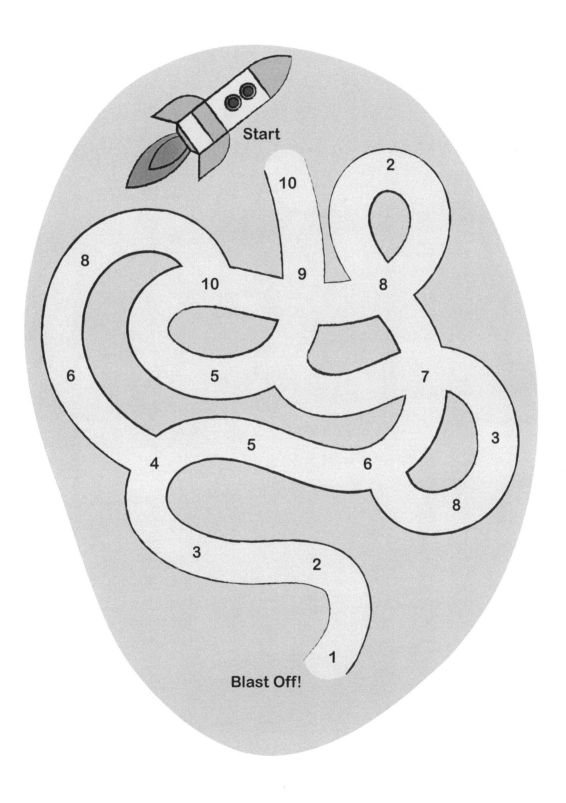

# Find the Fruits

How many of each type of fruit do you see in the grocery store? Write the numbers in the boxes at the top of the next page.

# Answer Key

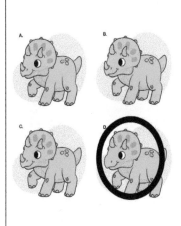
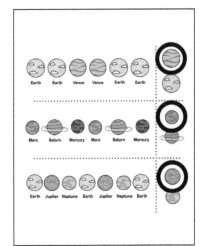

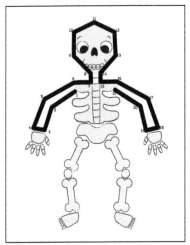
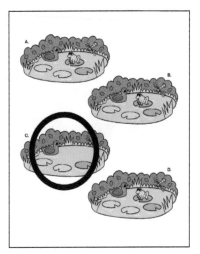

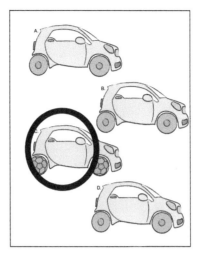

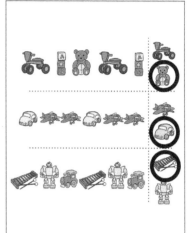

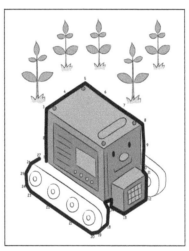

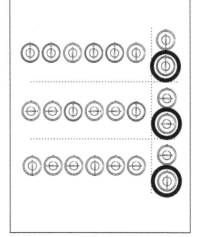

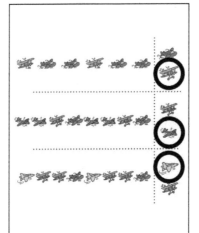

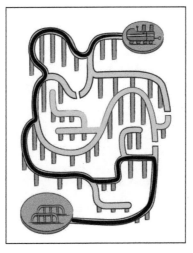

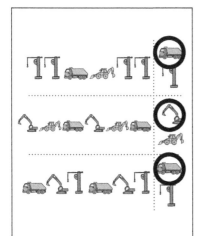

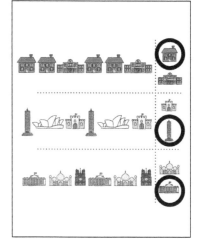

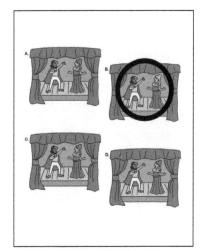

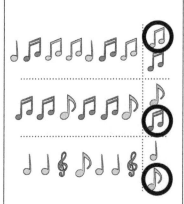

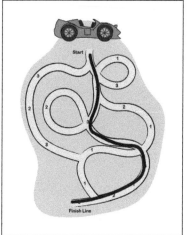

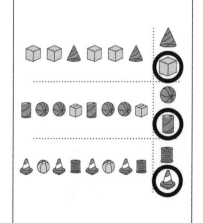

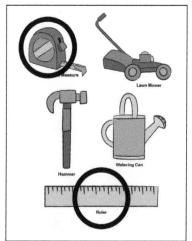

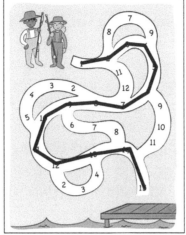

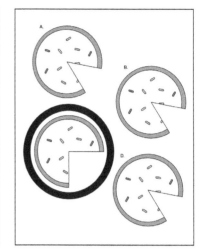

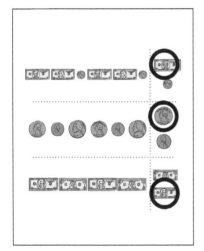

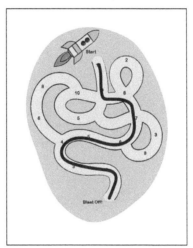

# About the Author

**Mandisa Watts** is a CPA/MBA, mother of three (including twins), and the founder of Happy Toddler Playtime, an online resource for parents, teachers, and caregivers, showcasing open-ended and child-led activities and crafts. There, Mandisa shares her kid-approved, colorful playtime activities that involve art, sensory play, and construction. Mandisa is also the author of *Exciting Sensory Bins for Curious Kids*. You can find more fun and engaging activity ideas at HappyToddlerPlaytime.com.

CPSIA information can be obtained
at www.ICGtesting.com
Printed in the USA
LVHW021616250621
691137LV00003B/9

9 781648 768644